10 OPEN ADOPTION ESSENTIALS

10 OPEN ADOPTION ESSENTIALS

RUSSELL ELKINS

10 Open Adoption Essentials
What Children Need Their Adoptive Parents and Birthparents to Know About Open Adoption Relationships
part 1 of the series: 30 Minute Guides to Headache-Free Open Adoption Parenting
By Russell Elkins
©2019 Russell Elkins

series line editors: Kim Foster, Jenna Lovell
series content editors: Martin Casey, Cathy Watson Childs

Cover photo and author photo by Jammie Elkins Photography
Cover design by Inky's Nest Design
Interior book layout by Inky's Nest Design

ISBN: 978-1-950741-05-2

Inky's Nest Publishing

RussellElkins.com
2nd edition
First edition printed in 2012 in the United States of America

CONTENTS

1

HOPEFUL ADOPTIVE PARENTS SHOULD NEVER FEEL ENTITLED

My wife and I went to a conference once that had a question and answer session with a panel of birthparents. One of the birthmothers had placed a baby for adoption a few years earlier and was again pregnant at the time. She was considering, but still undecided, about placing this child for adoption as well. After the class finished, a lot of the hopeful adoptive parents in the room swarmed her like wasps at a picnic. I could see the discomfort written on her face as couples batted their eyes and turned on their charm to ensure she would remember them if she did choose adoption. I am sure she remembered them, but perhaps not in a good way.

This is a tough balance to find for a lot of people. On one hand it is important for hopeful adoptive parents to get their names and faces out into the adoption world as much as possible. The process can take years and years for a lot of couples, especially for those who do not work to make sure their presence is available. On the other hand, pressuring potential birthparents is never a good idea. Expecting parents considering adoption already feel pressure about their decision.

When considering adoption and choosing an adoptive couple, what potential birthparents need is support, not pressure. Ultimately, the decision is meant to be on the shoulders of the birthparents, not on anybody else. Their own family and friends can (and should) give input and influence, but they should not pressure them into making a decision that is not right for them.

It is common for the potential birthparents' family and friends to feel like the baby should stay in their circle. Many times an aunt or a grandma will offer or even insist on raising the child so the baby can stay in the family. Also, because most people know of a couple who has trouble with infertility, it is quite possible the expecting parents are pressured to place the child with them. While placing a child with someone they are already close to is not uncommon and works out well for many, it is not for everybody. It will change their relationship. That does not mean it will necessarily change for the worse, but the relationship will always be different than it was before.

Hopeful adoptive couples should never feel entitled to someone else's baby. This is easier said than done for a lot of people because the thing they want most in this world—to begin or add to their family—is something that leaves them very much at the mercy of other people. Even when a couple has been contacted and chosen to adopt a child, that child is not their child yet. Even if the child has come home with them, the couple still does not have the right to feel entitled to this child. Once everything has been finalized through the courts, then and only then does the couple get to claim that child as theirs. Up until that day, all decisions regarding placement or well-being of the child are still in the hands of the biological parents, and they are well within their rights to change their mind.

2

When my wife and I went through the adoption process for the first time, we did not really know what we were getting ourselves into. We knew we were committing to something big when we decided to have our adoptions be open, but we did not truly understand the dynamics of it.

We did not know our son's birthmother before she first contacted us five months into her pregnancy, but we quickly began the process of getting to know each other. I have heard people compare those early contacts to when a couple is first courting. The expecting mother was getting to know us while we were doing our best to impress her, and vice versa. It is not that our relationship was superficial or fake, because it was not, but just like with any other relationship, the deeper we got into the relationship, the more we understood each other and were able to intimately work together.

Adoption, especially open adoption, is a crazy roller coaster ride of emotions. At one point my wife and I were on top of the world, and at other times we were nervously biting our fingernails down to nubs. The process was just as intense for our children's birthparents. The difficult thing with adoption, however, was that our emotions were often opposite one another. Sometimes the very things that brought us joy were the same things that brought the birthparents stress and pain. We were up while they were down. And sometimes it worked the same way in reverse; they were up while we were down.

We were on the ride together, though. When we signed up for open adoption, we wanted to be in it for the long haul, not just the easy times. In that sense, it is kind of like a marriage. The open adoption relationship is not one that can be taken lightly and easily cut off if things get uncomfortable. Things will get uncomfortable, especially during the first year. That is almost certain. The adoptive side needs to work side-by-side with the biological parents in order to understand each other. It can be very difficult to understand what the other side is going through. If one side is only concerned about themselves—failing to consider the difficulty, sacrifice or pain from the other side—the relationship is going to suffer.

Just like within any marriage, communication is number one. It is not a matter of just one side understanding the other. It is a matter of both sides understanding each other, which can be difficult when neither side will likely ever be in the other's shoes. An important key with communication is understanding that the relationship and situation will change as time goes on. That is inevitable. Things will change as the child gets older and is able to make his or her own decisions. Things will change as both sides begin again to get on with regular life. Things will change yet again if the birthparents get married and start their own families. The important thing is to realize these things, expect them to fluctuate, and continue to be willing to roll with those differences.

If the relationship is not nurtured, it will fall apart. It always helps to hear someone say "thank you" for the sacrifices being made because both sides are making them. When both sides work together, everyone involved is better off, stronger and happier than they would be otherwise.

3

BIRTHPARENTS & ADOPTIVE PARENTS BOTH NEED THE OPPORTUNITY TO HEAL

It is probably obvious to everybody that the birthmother will need to heal from the difficulty of placing a child for adoption. God hardwired it into our mortal bodies to be that way. It can be very difficult and overwhelming for a woman to carry a child inside of her for the majority of a year, then place that child into someone else's arms after going through the painful process of delivery.

The birthmother is not the only one who needs to heal, though. The forgotten person in a lot of adoptions is the birthfather. For whatever reason, it is not uncommon for him to be excluded from the decision-making process by the birthmother or by others. It is important for everybody, especially the adoptive parents, to note that many men are just as emotionally invested in the pregnancy and adoption process as are the women, and they should not be brushed aside if they would like to also be involved. It is more common for a man to step away from the adoption than it is for a woman, but communication is the only way for adoptive couples to know if he is removed by choice or whether he felt compelled. He may or may not want to receive updates and pictures along with the birthmother.

It is also very important to note that adoptive couples need to heal. This concept is beyond comprehension for a lot of people, but it is very common. After all, adoptive parents are the ones receiving the gift of parenthood—the greatest gift one person could give another, right? Getting that gift, however, comes about by being on the receiving end of one of the most painful things the birthparents may go through in their lives. Knowing that their joy came from someone else's pain—especially since that pain is on the shoulders of someone the adoptive couple loves so much—often causes a lot of guilt for the adoptive couple. The more open the adoption is, the more difficult it can be for the adoptive parents to know the birthparents are hurting from the separation.

Birthparents are making a huge sacrifice. Nobody denies that. The adoptive couple should find comfort and relief from their guilt in knowing they are doing their very best to provide the one thing the birthparents want most—providing the best care and love possible for the child.

Understanding that both sides hurt and both sides need to heal is vital for a healthy open adoption relationship. If one side refuses to accept another person's pain, then their own pain will be much harder to overcome, increasing (instead of decreasing) the stress in the relationship. Communication is the only way to help the other side see all aspects. When hurting, it can be all too easy to forget that other people are hurting as well, which is never a good thing.

My wife and I have helped our children's birthparents heal by being willing to listen to their concerns and needs. We have done our best to give them the contact and the tools they need to work things out in their way.

Our children's birthparents have helped us heal as well. The most important thing they have done has been to communicate to us that they approve of the way we are parenting. They have done this through words as well as actions. Perhaps nothing has been more important to us than this in our own healing process.

4

JEALOUSY ISSUES MUST BE
ADDRESSED & RESOLVED

After my wife and I began to discuss having children, it was fun to imagine her belly growing larger and larger as we came closer to the day when we would be parents. We imagined all the physical discomfort, juggling of hormones and pain that would accompany the pregnancy and delivery.

It seems funny to feel like we have missed out on something when the physical process of having kids is some of the worst physical discomfort and pain a woman could go through. I know that seeing my wife in that much pain would probably be even harder on me than if I were going through it myself. And yet, even though we know it is difficult, we still wish there was a way we could have gone through it at least once. Plus, it never helps that other mothers seem to bring up their pregnancy or delivery just about every time parenthood comes up in conversation. A lot of adoptive couples feel jealousy toward other people for their ability to experience these things, even sometimes directing those jealousies toward their children's birthparents.

Another common reason for jealousy among adoptive parents is knowing that their children do not share their DNA. My children's genes are not my genes. My son has his birthmother's beautiful eyes and my daughter has her birthfather's chin, both of which I will never be able to claim. If someone were to look at my children and notice that they do not look like me, would they not connect her to me in the same way as they would if we did look alike? Those are jealousy issues adoptive parents sometimes need to overcome.

The flip side of the coin should be obvious. Birthparents often feel jealousy because someone else gets to have the experience of spending each day with the child they gave birth to, a child that has their eyes or complexion. Birthparents will not be there to kiss a booboo or watch the child get on the school bus for the first time. That privilege belongs to the adoptive couple.

Jealousy is a common issue for both sides to deal with in open adoption. The more open the adoption relationship, the more we can see what the other has that we cannot have ourselves. Dealing with these jealousies is not a matter of just getting over it. I have learned to *embrace* my role as an adoptive father through open adoption, not just accept it. I am proud of who and what I am. I am proud of how I get to help my children and help their birthparents. When I became able to embrace these things, I actually learned to enjoy the thought of letting our children's birthparents claim some things we cannot.

Both sides cannot live through each other in order to fill the void. It will not work.

5

When emotions start running high, it is easy to lose track of rationality. Adoption, especially open adoption, can be a battlefront between the rational mind and the emotional mind. Hopeful adoptive couples know what they want, and they know they want it as soon as they can get it. They know that being contacted by a potential birthparent is a big deal, and if something causes it to fall through, they may rightfully worry it will be a long time before they get the opportunity again. That is never a good excuse for hopeful adoptive parents to make promises they will not keep just to try to ensure an adoption will not fall through.

The bottom line is there are going to be a lot of things taking place that both sides do not anticipate. Even though my wife and I had already gone through the process once, with our second adoption we experienced things we did not anticipate. There is nothing wrong with that. We were fortunate enough that we had our heads on straight, and we were able to figure things out as we went along without promising things we did not know we could deliver.

Hopeful adoptive parents owe it to birthparents to become as educated as possible about what they are getting themselves into. Granted, it is impossible to understand fully what is about to take place without having been there, and every adoption is different, but finding out as much as possible is the only way to make informed decisions.

Birthparents owe it to adoptive parents to learn as much as they can as well. It works both ways since the relationship will never be one-sided.

It is okay to say the words "I don't know" when dealing with uncertainties about the future. I cannot stress that enough.

It is important to take the time to decide what things can be promised for certain. For my wife and me, we knew we could promise pictures, and we knew we could promise to never cut them out of our life. We promised we would always be willing to communicate and try to work things out if problems came up between us. Those are very simple promises, and we have been able to keep them.

Keeping the promises simple is a good way to give leniency for change because, like stated before, things will change with time. With some open adoptions there is a need to make specific promises, such as in the case of when potential birthparents ask for a written agreement about the exchange of information. It is still very important to decide those things together and promise only what can be reasonably delivered. The relationship is never going to be damaged by delivering more than what was originally promised from either side, but promising something only to come up short later is always bad.

Remember that every relationship should be based on trust, and the quickest way to ruin that trust is to break promises. It is not like selling a car where the buyer is stuck with what they purchase after signing the papers. Adoption is legally binding, but the open relationship cannot be legally enforced.

Open adoption is a moral commitment, not a legal one.

6

I cannot count the number of times I have rolled my eyes at people who tell me they understand what I am going through. People will say they understand our infertility predicament because it took them a year to get pregnant instead of a month or two like everybody else. That is a start, but it is not quite the same thing. A man once told me he understood what it was like to place a child for adoption because he was really attached to his nephew who had to move across the country. I'm sorry, but no. That is not the same thing.

Sometimes people will say really insensitive or ignorant things about adoption, especially about open adoption. That's okay. It's not the end of the world. Most people who step on our toes do not realize they are doing it. Not only do they fail to realize they are being insensitive, but most of the time they

27

are actually trying to be helpful or friendly. There are a lot of things people do not understand unless they have been there themselves.

Most people have not experienced adoption, so most people do not know that adoption has changed drastically over the last few decades. It was not very long ago that adoption was avoided in conversation. On top of that, open adoption is a very young concept. A lot of people still cannot understand why we would want to do adoption this way.

It is important to allow people a little slack when they slip up with their words. Very few people outside the adoption community know what terminology to use or what not to say. Nobody, even people within the adoption community, is exempt from tripping over words. I have had to put my own foot in my mouth a few different times because of my inability to see something sensitive. When something is especially important to us, like being parents or starting a family, we tend to be more sensitive than we otherwise would be. If we let those sensitivities rule our lives, we will fall into the adoption traps of the past when people avoided the topic altogether.

When things get difficult, it is nice to find a social network. One of the most common ways of networking with like-minded people is on the internet. Facebook is a good place to find some of these, as are blog sites. On these pages, we are able to talk about topics, ask one another for opinions, and confide in each other about the difficulties of open adoption. It is an incredible tool for connecting with people who understand and care.

7

ADOPTED CHILDREN CAN BE TOLD THEIR HISTORY IS THROUGH AN ACT OF LOVE

I am a better man because of what being a father has taught me, and I am a better man because of what open adoption has taught me. My wife is a better woman for the same reasons. Our children's birthparents are also better people because of what they have gone through. Our focus is not on us, though. It is on our children.

My first goal with open adoption is to help my children understand that they came to our home through an act of love from their birthparents, not from abandonment. I want them to be able to embrace their history rather than just learn to accept it. The best way I know how to help make that happen is to show them how much we love and respect their birthparents. If they are able to see our love for them, we believe they will be more likely to follow that up with their own love.

Having that love for their birthparents will make it easier to embrace their story like we do.

My children have a unique family tree. Their birthparents are not just people we love. They are family. Our children's birthparents care about all of us, not just the child who shares their genes. Whenever they come to visit, they visit all of us and their love for everyone in our home shows. As long as the relationship stays healthy, I cannot see how letting other people love our children could do anything but help them see how important they are to the world.

Every adoption is different, though, and so is every relationship that comes along with them. Even more important is to take into account that every child is different. As our children grow older, they will be able to better express their minds and make decisions for themselves. If my wife and I are ever encouraging something with adoption that they do not want, it will be important for us to respect their wishes. After all, everybody involved wants what is best for the child. If my children want to see their birthparents less than my wife and I want them to, how will we handle that? If they want to see their birthparents more than we want them to, how will we handle that?

We have grown especially fond of our children's birthparents. They are the type of people we would invite to our home even if we were not connected through the lives of our little ones. Our relationship will never be the same type of relationship we have with our other family members or friends down the street, though. We do not clean the house spotless when my brother comes to visit for the weekend like we might when a birthparent comes to visit. We do not spend the extra time to make sure our children are wearing their absolute cutest outfit when my aunt comes over to see us. This intensity may fade a little with time, but we will always have it in the back of our minds to want to show the birthparents what a great decision they made by choosing us. That is human nature. There is nothing wrong with that, but the relationship may always be a little more formal than the other relationships in our life because of who we are to each other.

It is up to us adults to pay attention to how the children respond and to flow with that unique relationship. Our feelings are important, but the children need to come first.

8

Sharing pictures is a little different than we expected it to be before we adopted the first time. First of all, there are a million different ways to share pictures. Some people exchange photos through email or regular post. It is common for adoptive parents to let birthparents have access to their Facebook page or family blog. Other people, like my wife and I, have a separate blog set up just for posting pictures and updates about the adopted child and our family.

However the adoptive couple chooses to share pictures, their frame of mind changes with every click of the camera. Adoptive parents have a tendency to want to continually show the birthparents that they made the right decision to choose them, and every photo is a window into the adoptive home. We try a little extra hard to look our best in those pictures. Not only that, but pictures are usually expected with some sort of regularity with open adoptions. No matter if pictures are shared once a day or once a decade, it is not the same as sharing pictures with my other family members.

At first, it felt almost like we were being monitored. The birthparents were not doing something to make us feel that way, but just the act of sending them pictures made us feel a little bit like someone was checking up on us. Nobody likes to feel that way, but as time went by and as the birthparents showed us that they supported and sustained us as the parents, sharing pictures not only became easier, but also became something enjoyable.

It is hard to know exactly how often and what to share. Some open adoptions have that decision made prior to finalizing, expecting it to happen once a month, once a year, or however often. With a lot of adoptions, like ours, the frequency has changed. In the beginning we posted photos a lot, and as time has gone by, pictures are not shared as often. That was by design and was something we discussed with the birthparents. We knew they would have a great need for pictures early on, so we were willing to help out with that need. As time passed, our relationship became more comfortable, which meant that sharing pictures felt less like we were checking in. We enjoy sharing photos now even though it can be time consuming.

Face-to-face meetings can be much more stressful than any other form of contact. My wife and I were insecure about our adoption relationship in the early stages. We did not know how the birthmother would handle the visit. Such personal contact between everybody involved can stir up intense emotions and insecurities for everyone. As time went by and as we worked together on our roles and relationships, those feelings changed. Even now, years later, there are days that are harder than others, but feelings change and things get easier.

I recommend keeping the first visits as simple as possible. Invite only those closely connected to the birthparents. For some adoptive couples, it can be very healing and beneficial to involve the extended birth family members. For others, inviting extra people only adds stress. For the adoptive couples who do choose to involve extended family and friends, it can be a good idea to keep the first meeting or two small to ensure that things stay comfortable.

It can go the other way as well. Some adoptive couples enjoy inviting birthparents to meet the extended adoptive family. My wife and I choose not to do this because we like to have our family and friends connect our children directly to us and not think of someone else first. We do not feel like our relationship is lacking by not involving our family in our adoption relationship, but I do know a lot of people who enjoy having their family circles intertwined in that way. The choice should be made according to the needs of the relationship.

These decisions need to be addressed *before* the needs arise. If the adoptive parents promise to send pictures but no specifics are laid out, then the birthparents may expect photos once a week while the adoptive couple plans to send them once a month. This concept is true for all forms of contact.

A disconnect like this can only further complicate an already complex relationship. Discussing these things beforehand and coming to decisions on the specifics on all forms of contact will remove unneeded stress from future interactions.

9

ADOPTIVE PARENTS SHOULD BE CAREFUL TO OPEN THE DOOR SLOWLY

Adoptive parents often feel a desire to give the birthparents the world. After all, the birthparents gave them the gift of parenthood—possibly the greatest gift a human being could give another, right? After time, however, life settles down. Where does that leave the relationship between the birthparents and adoptive parents? If adoptive parents promise the world, they will not be able to deliver it, even if they want to. On top of that, having a desire to give everything will wear the adoptive couple out. Feeling like they have to give everything tends to feel the same as feeling like they are in perpetual debt. A person can only endure the feeling of being so deeply in debt for so long before they want to find a way to escape it. If the feeling is so deep that they do not feel like they can ever get out from under it, what choices will they make?

The period of time between when the adoptive couple is chosen and when placement occurs is an intense time of emotion. My wife and I spent a lot of time trying to figure out what we were feeling and deciding what we wanted to do. Once the baby was born, those feelings did not get any easier. They just changed into different things to worry about. Things do get easier with time, but that first year is usually much more stressful than the following ones. The relationship is still being molded by everybody involved, and everybody needs to adjust.

It is okay for the level of openness to change with time. In fact, I consider that a good thing. It is a good idea to start with things the adoptive couple is sure they can handle and progress from there.

Communication is the key. Even though it is more than okay to say "I do not know" when trying to plan for the future, it is a good idea to try to figure out some sort of structure everyone is comfortable with. If there is no structure, both sides are going to start acting on what they assume is the proper level of interaction, and the odds of those two sides being exactly the same are pretty slim.

It is much easier to start out smaller and open a relationship more and more with time than it is to try to work backward. This can be tough since the most intense feelings are at the beginning, and the early stages can require the most frequent interaction. But if the birthparents are accustomed to a certain level of openness, and the adoptive couple decides they are becoming exhausted and need to step back, it is not easy to do so without risking damage to the relationship.

Again, it is much easier to open a relationship more and more with time than to work backward. Relationships are not damaged by delivering more than what is expected, especially if both sides feel comfortable with approaching the relationship slowly.

10

If there is one thing that I have learned with open adoption, it is that absolutely nothing is universal. There is no topic or opinion that everybody can truly agree upon one hundred percent. Even everything discussed here in this book that I state matter-of-factly is open for debate. Nothing is universal.

There are all types of adoptions. Even within open adoption there are all types of relationships. Some open adoptions have regular face-to-face visits while others never do. There is absolutely nothing wrong with that. Every person considering adoption, whether on the adoptive side or biological side, needs to take a step back and decide what they want for their own situation. Just as birthparents are the ones who need to make the decision whether or not to place a child for adoption, adoptive couples are the only ones who can truly know what to decide for their own home. If a closed adoption is what their home needs, there is nothing wrong with that (as long as they never promise an open relationship, of course). There are birthparents out there who want a closed adoption as well.

Every adoption is different. Every relationship between birthparents and adoptive parents is different. The relationship my wife and I have with the birthparents of our son is different than the relationship we have with the birthparents of our daughter. There is nothing wrong with that. It is important not to try to be something or someone else.

When I wrote the book *Open Adoption, Open Heart* I made an effort to just tell everything my wife and I went through. I made no attempt to tell others what they will feel. My goal was let the reader come along for the ride so that they could ponder how they would feel if they were in our shoes as they experienced our adoption alongside us.

Even within an adoptive couple's relationship, there are differences. I am obviously a man, and my wife is obviously a woman. Our minds do not work the same way. We process things differently. Sometimes I feel stronger about something than she does, and sometimes she feels stronger about something than I do. We cannot expect one another to feel the same way about everything. That is the true with any relationship, but adoption tends to magnify those differences.

Adoption often brings together people who might never cross each other's paths. It is a great opportunity to develop unique relationships that cannot be experienced anywhere else in life. With those unique relationships we learn new ways of loving. I am a better person because of those differences and because of those relationships. Open adoption is one of the best things to happen to us, and we have never regretted choosing an open relationship.

www.ingramcontent.com/pod-product-compliance
Lightning Source LLC
Chambersburg PA
CBHW071938020426
42331CB00010B/2924